NeoSoul poetry ATX

est. 2005

The
Anthology

From The Pens Of NeoSoul Poetry Slam

vol: one

by
The Poets of NeoSoul

Edited by Sunni Soper & October Brown
Cover Design by Christopher Michael

Released: March 2017

Published by:

Printed in the United States of America
ISBN 0-9984270-2-0
Published by 310 Brown Street
www.310brownstreet.com
310brownstreet@gmail.com
neosoulslam@gmail.com

The Pens Of NeoSoul Poetry Slam

DEDICATION

This book is dedicated to the voices that have touched the NeoSoul stage. To all the Souldiers past and present. To every ear that paused to listen. To the fallen, Shelia, Shannon and Queen Pen.

GRATITUDE

To our sister slam, Austin Poetry Slam, thank you for all the support and love.

The Pens Of NeoSoul Poetry Slam

ARE YOU REDAY FOR THE NEXT POET?

ABOUT THE STORMS

We are a people accustomed to drowning
In a flood of depth and debt
With not enough money and too much rain.
For most in the Philippines, this is life.
When the tourists come,
They love our hospitality,
Our food
And our women.

The tourists
they stay just long enough to take a picture;
loving how the green in their pockets
Stretches as far as the green of the trees dressing the
mountains;
endless evidence that the rain came yesterday,
is coming today,
and will come again tomorrow.
Then, they come home
post their pictures on Facebook,
talk about the heat,
the smell,
the food,
and say how beautiful everything was that they left behind.

In the meantime,
the news in America shows a battered house with a woman and
child
sitting on top of what was their roof once,
as if to say we are above this destruction.
I still hear it in the way my father speaks,
when he opens his mouth
how our native tongue, almost refuses to talk of the tragedy
in a language, other than its own birthright.
"Bumaha nanaman sa Pilipninas"
There was another flood in the Philippines,
rolls out of the tired thunder in his throat
as fast as a siren passes by,
or a bicycle flying past in the middle of a storm.
His words linger like the smell after it rains.

There is always too much rain.

The house I was raised in does not recognize how I have grown.
But it knows where the flood stopped
by how high the water has marked the walls on the first floor.
It was past my height the day I left at eleven years old.
To think, if we had stayed, I could have drowned in my own home.
My uncles are grateful that the house is still standing;
that the roof has kept its head.
that the car is still running even after it was swallowed,
that they had enough food to swallow while riding out the storm,
that the dog was good enough swimmer,
that since two floods ago, there is not that much left for other to steal.

They don't turn on the TV because it might attract thieves.
They don't turn on the TV because the power is out.
The power is out so they take batteries from a flashlight to turn the radio on.
They don't listen that long so they won't eat in the dark.
The matches are for cooking.
The candles are too wet.
They are used to this.
That land of my fathers',
that land of mine
is a beautiful country.
She is the child of typhoons and hurricanes.
She is well loved by the rain
It is a country of substance and it comes from suffering
drenched in yet another wet season
with barely enough time to dry in.

Shivering in the flood water
Like a house on stilts
Whose legs have been weathered
thin as a fisherman's pole,
but still bent on snapping back.

7

We are a people accustomed to drowning.
Until you are gasping for breath,
you have yet to see a storm

Jomar Valentin

AN ODE TO MR. CATFISH

Oh Mr. Catfish,
Cube shaped temple of fried delight.
Red light district for the nose, mouth and ears.
Eastside icon of deep south cooking,
Heaven for the senses…

Mr. Catfish...
Thank you for the… catfish.
Thank you for the chicken strips in sets of 4 and 6.
Thanks for the beer and margarits,
Thanks for the fried shrimp OR oysters,
Thanks for the gumbo,
I want an extra-large.

Thanks for the boudin links,
Thanks for the boudin balls,
Thanks for the cheesy boudin balls.

Thanks for the fries.
They are perfectly fried...
Thanks for the catsup,
Thank you for the honey mustard.
Thank you for the plastic ramekins the honey mustard comes
in…
Thank you for the extra helping of heart you put into all the food
you serve.

I've never gotten a strand of hair in my food here,
But if i did… I would eat it.
And it would be delicious.
And hopefully fried.

Mr. Catfish, I like both cats and fish,
Yet you are better than either of those animals individually,
Dare I say it…

9

Austin NeoSoul

You are better than Whataburger.
I love you as much as I love Cheez-Its,
Which is a lot.

Thank you for staying open 2 hours late for us every single
Thursday night.
For being a home to not just food,
But our community as well.

Thank you for calling my number,
Mr. Catfish, you always have my number…
Whether or not I remember that number,
I remember when you kept calling that number and I didn't hear
it,

And when you finally found me,
You said, "Thank God, I thought you had left."
Well thank God for you Mr. Catfish,
I hope you never leave.

AR-SAHARA (SAHARA)

With every breath that we breathe, may we be ever aware of the Divine Presence, the Source of all that we receive.

bismillah al rahman al rahim
I remember when we spoke in earth and dirt….
we were so close to life,
that death stuck tightly to the back of our throats.
and when we swallowed we could
still taste the saline in God's sweat;
the grace of his work
attached to the moisture in the air,
and the wells of raindrops.
existence was an afterthought,
heaven hid slightly behind the lids of our eyes,
and we remembered the ringing in our ears were not annoyances;
but insistences from angels who'd come and gone long before us…
and we listened…
no thought was shallow
every utterance, grave…
each word sliced
our tongue and cheek
coated our lungs and cut our lips.
our blood red tinted sentences were spat and delivered with a sense
of urgency …
like the air we breathe
we pulled pathos in and out
out and in in and out
again, and again
savoring contemplation's birth
as we knew it would embody the spirit
long after we transcended
and returned to ashes and dust
gas and light
when our remains became another lifetime of memories to conceive.
we spoke purposefully with purpose,
never knowing if it would be our last or first…
silence a confidant,
clandestinely denying the defiance
of loose lipped prophets
who knew not what they heard

11

or learned or read or said.
simply liars out to tell a story that was never theirs to tell…

do you remember,
when soil stained teeth hid
secret languages and slanguages
smiles were yells across cavernous chasms
echoed from the heart beats of our unborn children's children
as if our words held their world in our hands
as ours had been carefully sculpted and molded
in the crinkled palms and psalms of our great grand's grand's?
can you remember?
when we spoke in earth and dirt
there no false poets spewing blasphemy from cursed souls;
no wicked pandering from the curiosities of the weak at mouth…
their words fell deaf at the feet of our wisdom...
we shook the dust of those who did not welcome us,
our teachings or preachings…
there were no thunderous applause or claps of hands,
simply thunder clapping, clasping the night
grinding the darkness into sparks of light…
we didn't aspire to be stars
we were demi-gods.
half human, half prose
and we spoke for nothing more than worship and survival.
these poetry joints were as sacred as church revivals,
we religiously penned our lives in soot and sand,
G.O.D.'s blood our ink, our minds, his scroll
if I can no longer spit in prayer,
then Neo-Soul take my pen, cuz
this is my last….
Amin

kdtaylor, 2010
section 8 coffee

BATTLEFIELDS

Eyes reflect both his said and unspoken stories
truth lives somewhere between
the storyteller and the observer

My son peers at me with beautiful brown eyes
looking to me for all the answers
even when he's unsure of the questions
I wish-I want to have them
usually...I don't
or I do
but can't share them

He doesn't know he's in a war zone
or that his existence sparked the course
words of love and adoration
become the cotton that clouds his ear
from angry gunfire
shots stolen in the dark
stabs at character
love can be a mighty weapon
please don't let it be our downfall
Please don't let it be his

Despite our good intentions
he will ultimately be our fallen soldier
in a battle he never asked for
afraid to break him too soon
fearing the blitz that may follow
the slam of a judge's gavel

Do I tell him now or later?
Does either option pose any favors
to the way his world will tilt differently
Will sun rays still be as bright for him?

13

Austin NeoSoul

Will he remember visions of the world

at arms out, face dirty, foot level?
Dust flecked in irises
Brush yourself off
stand at your tallest

Mommy's sorry to be part of your fall, son
Know I'll always be here to pick you up
Forgive my mistakes,
As I stumble through
Trying to "fight the good fight"
knowing those words were first spoken
just to cushion their reality

I worry that hints of darkness
following bouts of lost innocence
lie cool just beneath the warmth of his skin

I can tell he senses the pull
He's not quite sure where the current's coming from
he clings to two lifeboats,
Not realizing each is being steered
by opposing commander in chiefs
Arrogantly trying to decide
what's best for him
between tightened strands of ignorance
and our inability to call a truce
and truly put him first

How can we see this so differently?
How can we see HIM so differently?

Please, I don't want to hate his father
he's our baby, blueprinted in our union
love now dissolved
lays bitter in the back of throats

14

struggling through acidic niceties
This-THIS is biological warfare at its pinnacle

And as with any war-torn people-
Is there ever really a winner
or justice
when those of us,
judges and lawyers,
fathers and mothers
leave less scathed
than the innocent who have fallen
to the battles of custody.

My son has been enlisted since the day he was born,
Been on the front lines ever since,
As president of this misery,
I release you from active duty,
Resume to playgrounds, and fields of innocence.
Mommy's got it from here.

©2008 Sarah J Uphoff

BLACK/MLK

I prefer Black, African American takes up too much space.
Bring the Negro back, the ones that fought for freedom.
Now the brown skinned felons with no right to vote, you don't
even count so you have no freedom.

We are unfinished, in the raw, butt naked
Changing clothes often 'cause our community is too big
That Nigga mentality got the churches of Chicago filled with
revivals that last a long time, unnecessary funerals, and
depreciated human life is black faded.
A Commercial for life.
Stay tuned in and not turned off.

We don't rent rims
We look for backboards; your back bone is needed
Get the twinkles out of your toes and plant yourself
We have a history of superlative roots.
Roots that have sprouted, breaking ground.
Don't be uprooted, you better love your beautiful self

Botox cannot erase these lines, No facelift can uplift you.
Empower or Empire? We have shit to do.
Make you words count, how high can your words count? Think
of yourself blessed.
I've never seen a real tanning bed deliberately

browning yourself
"YOU CAN'T HANDLE THE BLACK"
"So I wanna be black, But like I really don't wanna be Black"
Local owned store owned by a completely different race
BUT, they can sell you the best Nappy
Get your weaves starting at $300
SOLD, to the next mother with food stamps, 10 kids and 5
babies' fathers

16

Throwing around my taxes like change isn't needed

Collagen is not needed for my mother's lips to tell stories of
hard work.
She remembers the "White Only" signs hung like a real piece of
art.
Words with arrows for an intended target.
Cotton balls and blue crayons are all we need to see clear
skies.
That's how easy it is to love us.

Keep your picket signs in your back pockets.
It's possible problems need paid attention.
Martin Luther King – Slam Poet 1962
What was it like to sacrifice life for a perfect 10?
So powerful, the highest score was death.
Words can get you killed.
Rest peaceful slam Champ.

Have you ever slammed to death?
Speaking up with confidence wrapped around your

neck.

Quit waiting on "Getting by" 'cause he really never shows up.
We give words so much power, so when they come down
heavy,
prepare for the outcome
Make words weigh in pounds for power.
Black goes with everything.
Misconceived like it makes you look small

Move your people
Let your words hang nooses
And color the whites black
Take your voice back
Get your priorities together

17

We are Words threading needles, stitching trying to keep ourselves together
We have to do better.
If you have absolutely nothing to fight for,
Then you are absolutely, nothing

La Love Robinson, 2010

THE DUNG BEETLE

Dung beetles were worshipped
by the ancient Egyptians.
Who thought the earth was a giant ball of dung
getting rolled across the sky.

Dung beetles don't drink water
poop has all the moisture they need.

Baby dung beetles are birthed
within poop balls which they then eat
as they grow larger. In some cases
the male and female will help each other
in creating the ball. It's really kind of cute
if you forget it's poop.

In the hot Sahara, dung beetles use poop
to keep themselves cool and regulate temperatures.
It's too complex for me to explain in this poem.

Dung beetles were introduced in Australia
to help agriculture. Normal poop stays above the surface
and it smells, and carries disease, and breeds flies.
But with dung beetles, oh what a difference.
The poop is buried, releasing nutrients into the soil,
decreasing populations of bush flies and then
acting as a nursery for more dung beetles.
And only good things happen from there.

New Zealand is studying introducing dung beetles
to combat methane gasses released by poop
and thus, fight global warming.
A dung beetle can bury 250 times its weight in an evening.
But not eat more than twice its weight in a day.
What an ecological saint.

19

(Too bad one of their most feared predators is agricultural pesticides.)

Oh, and they can fly.
No wonder the Egyptians revered dung beetles.

Wish I had my shit together.

Jacob Dodson

Haiku Interlude

Oh great Dung Beatle
I beseech you to help get,
my shit together

~Christopher Maiku

BUTTERFLY

I'm a changed person now...
I am no longer the caterpillar you once knew...
This beautiful butterfly has broken the cocoon...
And spread her wings... Do you see me?
In hues of lavender, turquoise and gold...
I am a beauty beyond anything you could ever imagine...
I bring blessings when I land on your shoulder...
I have surpassed spreading just plain luck...
The object of one's affection...
Too wonderful to be captured and caged...
Butterfly lovers allow me to float freely into the indigo sky...
I flutter...
Compared to a snow flake that has fallen so softly,
I am truly one of a kind...
Bringing about gasps of awe, I astonish the world...
You remember who I used to be...
With coal tinted glasses you attempt to see me as I was...
I stand before you anew...
Meticulously removing the intellectual cataracts that has caused
you, to not realize who I truly am...
I have exceeded even my own expectations...
In this race called life we are not even...
We are running side by side because my friend...
I have lapped you continuously and this...
Is just where we meet again...
Stubbornly you refuse to believe a change has come about...
No longer am I the caterpillar whose legs you pulled off to
impede my progress...
Touch my wings continuously this butterfly will never lose
momentum I refuse...
While within my cocoon you mocked me...
Swore I'd arrive a dull gray moth...
Surprise...
Your wishes of failure never reached me...
Your thoughts of negativity were blocked...
I am what you said I would never be,

21

Beautiful, Happy, Successful...

Point your eyes towards the heavens and watch me soar...
Out of your reach, above your head, beyond your wildest dreams...
I have met him... the man you strive to be...
I've seen his face... he doesn't look like you...
The man you claim you are…
I have watched him grow from concrete...
I landed on the heart of a rose…
And from it I took his foundation..
On the concrete I placed it and he sprouted because of me...
He never needed a cocoon because he was never like you and I...
I cried tears of happiness and watered my seedling in the midnight hours...
I have created the man you wish you were without you ever taking notice...
While inside your own cocoon you wanted me to emerge defeated...
Don't ever waste your wishes... And make empty threats...
I bloomed glamorously…
And unfortunately… you transpired... into… a bigger caterpillar.

Miss. Lizz

EATING DISORDER NARRATIVE

One day, you will decide to measure your self-worth by a number on a scale and hunger will be a feeling that you call home. People will whisper about how good you look. They will ask you your secret and you will say, "cross my heart and hope to die I'll never tell." You will realize that you spend the weekends running miles on a treadmill and memorizing the number of calories in foods you don't even eat anymore. You'll notice that your friends don't invite you out anymore because you always say no because every outing involves food and you still won't tell that secret of yours. You will blackout and fall down a flight of stairs. You will cry when people rush around you not because it hurt but because you've been trying to disappear and you hate all the attention. IVs and blood draws will become routine, will feel normal, crazy will take on a new meaning as you beg the nurse or doctor or therapist or whoever is listening to let you go home because you're fine. You will be sitting at a counter in a place with doors that lock people in crying over ensure over bread over cake wishing you could get out without sounding an alarm wondering how your life went so wrong. You will realize that while you are here gaining weight talking about feelings learning behavioral therapy skills and always fucking eating that your friends are going to interesting classes getting new internships double dating at fancy restaurants and it will hurt. Everything will begin to feel like too much. You will start to fantasize about your demise count pills and hide them away write letters saying goodbye carve I'm sorry into your skin and when you fail this will be your ultimate rock bottom. You'll learn that if you're not recovering you're dying and you won't want to fight against recovery anymore. You'll fight for recovery for bring your own dish holiday parties drunken Saturday nights with delivery pizza tears over break ups into an ice cream bowl movie theater dates with shared popcorn. You'll fight for the moments that make life worth living and someday, you'll look up to a room full of people and tell them that someday is today that one day you wanted to die but

23

someday you didn't. That today, you ordered macaroni and cheese from a food truck and it tasted like living.

Shelby Rae

EMANCIPATION PROCLAMATION

Every poet knows that the secret to a great poem is what you say, how you say it and does it
really mean something to you. We poets also know that the first line of a poem can make all the
difference in the world. Because it needs to be unforgettable. Like that scene from *Aliens*. The
first line should leap out the poet's mouth. Alien wrap itself around the audience's ear and
literally plant a new idea or feeling into their soul...that one day will burst out of their chest,
through their shirts and into the rest of their lives. In other words it is supposed to be like really
good.
Well I struggled with trying to write the perfect first line for this poem...I kept writing and rewriting
and rewriting until I ended up with four that I kinda liked...but I couldn't choose one so I decided
to use them all...

One

for her 14th birthday she was given a surprise kidnapping with the gift of slavery wrapped in
rape with rust colored ribbons made of chains. Happy Slaveday...sweetie

Two

little girls who give head to men in lines are not worthy of headlines about men who take, rape
and murder them.

Three

Her story will never rise to the importance of being front page and above the fold. She can only
assume the position of being front folded beneath the importance of his rise.

Four

this poem is another Flint Michigan story...
but this time water is a metaphor for a 14-year-old black girl,
the contamination is a metaphor for the black man and woman who raped her into the life of
human trafficking and
governor Snyder and the other grossly negligent Michigan officials who turned a blind eye to this
environmental and immoral hazard are metaphors for you and I for turning a blind eye to human
trafficking because we want to believe that slavery ended with the emancipation proclamation.
13th Amendment in lieu of Emancipation Proclamation or in addition
He couldn't hear her screams because her legs were wrapped around his ears...
Her story was Buried beneath ads for cheap clothing and Memorial Day sales. See she was the
fine print that no one takes the time
to read about.
her rape filled teens you will have to skip the front-page news,
the sports and business sections until you finally stumble onto the metro/state. And then slowly
but surely, you must wade your attention in and around stories about arenas next to soccer
fields, or how a local boy misspells his way to the title, ...
And even when you discover her story you better bring a magnifying glass and your
imagination...because there is less about her courage to survive and more about the judge who

convicted her overseers..

There was nothing about whether or not she was ok?

Not one drop of ink was sacrificed in the writing of her story not one word on whether she made

it back home to Flint. If she was met at the airport by family and friends.

No Inquiring minds want to know; did she rush home to wash the filth of slavery off her skin with

the contaminated waters of Flint? Now that story will sell...

I just wanted to know is she in a warm place that will help comfort her from the cold reality of

being a 14 year old ex-slave, in America, in 2016? Or did they treat her like she was a Baylor rape victim

telling her you are safe now, it's time for you to move on and just get over it?

And why shouldn't she... we already have. I mean slavery that was yesterday's news and

nobody is interested in that...

~Brian "B-Fran" Francis

FEAR

I am asked to write about the birth of my demons.
To tell how fear is born, the way it came into existence.
I struggle myself to ink, strike through words,
crumble a hundred pages with FEAR written all over them.
Leaving me waist deep in torture.
Feel the blood lap itself under my skin.
Flood my body with every story that has ever consumed me.
Fear, must've been born like this - in tremble and strange sounds.
Must be a belly's echo with muffled screams slung all around.
Must be an artist.
Must be an international student
relearning everything that couldn't make its way across the ocean.
Fear must be an island.
Must be lonely growing lusciously.
Must've grown fangs and thorns and vines.
Must've wrapped itself in everything hard and hurt.
Must've strangled love until its eyes popped out.
Fear must be blind and touching everything.
Fear must have eight arms and three heads.
Must be a monster mating with itself multiple times
until it became a forest, a continent, a whole person, a place to live.
Fear must have a stubborn heart.
Must thump stress, speak creep, must haunt
your dreams, your goals, your happiness.
Fear be a bottom feeder, must scrape every last bit
of hope from your feet, must keep you stuck and graduated hater.
Fear must be a police officer with an empty weapon
after emptying his weapon inside the soul of a black body.
It must be a black mother's home with all these unarmed black bodies
walking around.
Fear, must be a nigga. And *everybody wanna be a nigga but don't*
nobody wanna be a nigga.
Shots fired. Yeah. Shots fired.
Yeah, fear must be balmy, coiled, beauty and exotic.
The only person of color in the whole room.
Must be a man calling out another man when misogyny forces its way
into his mouth.
Fear must be coming out but still having to pretend to be someone
else.
Must be a body in transition.

Must be permission for two women to kiss in public/for two men to hold hands.
Fear must be given.
Must be a law/must be in place to save the human race.
Fear is who we loving, fucking, and paying our tithes too.
Yes!
Fear is a God.
A religion.
Who we pray to.
And believe in.
Fear mustn't be uttered, admitted or claimed to faith in.
Fear must just be who fear be and how fear came about.

~Ebony Stewart

FOR THE GREY PARTS OF BALTIMORE

i.   They swarm and hum under the fluorescent trick, swell
     like flood rushed out the alley. All of them hooded spooks
     on howl. "Damn," I think, "I used to know them boys."
     Back on the block. Before they were apparitions. Bullet
     bags. Bricks against fists. Jigsaws. Before they became
     graffiti, before they were B b L l A a C c K k when they
     were just boys. Just bones and cartilage. Just boys before
     the nick and chomp. Just before the heat in this city got
     body. Got they bodies. Got they chests. Got under they
     skin for good.

ii.   Left unburied to rot, boys started to writhe on asphalt.
     Seethe in the shadows, seek out their ancestors, all the
     living and the lived and the lost, unburied. Started to cut
     out, started to haunt back road ditches and main
     highways, started to dig under cement for roots, call on
     Papa Legba. Seek a dénouement to their sentence and
     exile, though exile has started to sound sovereign. Like it
     was a gift or like it was a little air. A gift or a curse, to
     abandon downtown, a blessing absent the gris gris or
     absent the wool cut or absent a price on the head of this
     city for its many crimes. Like blood in the water, there ain't
     never enough evidence to prove anything but we all
     concur! There is a problem here. An aching in this asphalt
     for something.

iii. On the T.V. they are trying to explain this black body. How
     it happened. They want to explain the technique. Explain
     the stains on the floor of the van. Explain "Just a little
     banging around for about four seconds, you know."
     Explain the short stop at the grocery store. Explain the
     policy dammit and the irate and the shackles and explain

the policy for wild things. Explain how to hang a man with no rope. Explain how to use his own neck against him. Explain the policy and the shackles and all the wild things. But no one is listening. They can see it all in HD, how at the corner of North and Mount, someone made eye contact with a switchblade. Check the rap sheet. For sure, there is enough evidence now.

iv.   I got to wonder about those boys. When did they get so raw around the throat? I know they can't remember, now they been translated. Now they been conjured. Coaxed. Now they been named—Beasts. Now they bark at all the burning in the streets. Sob and howl on the walls around them. Like this the last place you can pray in public. Spray cans on hiss, they all got throats full of funeral wreaths now. I want to know what happened? How did they get here? Even with all that root work, down in the bloody house of gawd, over in the university, up in the YMCA, out in the prison yard and all over ESPN, even with all that journey and all them Grammys it seems as though they still need a little push, a little incentive to get hot, to inhale enough smoke to disappear.

v.   They've started to whimper. Started to lick the necks of their muted young. Started to whine when one gets loose, jumps over the fence and ends up on a sidewalk too far downtown. They've started pacing, nibbling on a pile of old newspapers, nibbling on the raw meat strewn across what was once their front yard, started to get angry. Started wondering where the meat comes from and who threw it here in the first place. Started to question its brown edges. (Where the babies at anyways?) Started to get out the gate. Started to get body. Get they bodies back. Pick up the dead and howl. They got this growl

31

down in the gut and they've started to click their tongues, started to pop and light. Reach up and tear at the roof. Get a little sun in here. "Get my son in here!" Make em' see him. Get to the feelin'. That too tired to pretend, too tired to take it again feelin'. Get to it. Get right down to it. Started saying "Shit. Anything and everything can burn, I imagine."

Faylita Hicks

HER SMILE
By Michelle Desiree

She wears steel-toed black combat boots
laced up to her heart
trying to avoid feeling the crap she walks through
the stench assaults her senses
remembers memories engraved within membranes of her soul
like…

Her alpha-
ovulating beats pulsing the air
conception of her comes into existence
wading in fluids of rejection
bathed in the baptism of survival
and I wonder what lies beneath her smile

She-
an original score written on torn parchment
In backdrops of smoky rooms and back alleys
tattooed on yesterday's regrets and tomorrow's sequels
bittersweet childhood caught off guard
a lifetime of nocturnal screams
through muted whispers
permeating the air like rancid perfume
her little girl tears fall…unnoticed
upon coloring book pages
mixing with purple blues of shattered dreams
spilling outside the lines
fallen star wishes
angel wing wishes
Grandmother's sanctuary wishes
she just wishes…

They-
sharing same blood
only to bleed her innocence in corners of shadowed basements

33

disguised as deceitful games
he swallows her adoration in delicious gulps
trying to feed his own self hatred
and I still wonder what lies beneath her smile.

Fast forward-
still a scared lil' girl with big girl dreams
searching for daddy's love in the arms of harm's way
she finds him
hitting her like a train wreck
literally
off track
relishes in his spirit-breaking fists
craving his venomous kisses

He-
a lil' boy himself
hiding within obscurity
playing the role of a man
only to become the understudy
she his co-star
memorizes her lines
even if the lines are only screams
still she was never heard
unacknowledged existence repeated daily like late night reruns
tears placed just right
makeup flawless
hiding the affection darkening her eye
swelling her lip
or bruising her cheek
right on script
humiliation becoming her Oscar
cries of bewilderment her Grammy
and I still wonder what lies beneath her smile

encroaching walls closing in
as ceilings and floors of her world
evaporate like the curling smoke of a long forgotten cigar

The Pens Of NeoSoul Poetry Slam

left smoldering between life-stained fingers
she had to hate him enough to love a lil' bit of herself
one forgotten piece on an old dusty shelf
hidden within the confines of self-worth
trying to reclaim her childhood
her innocence
her womanhood
desperation dilates pupils past yesterday
facing reflections of smiles
like shattered glass
slowly etching lines of forgiveness down her face
entangled within truth of lies
tucked away neatly in corners of a mask
masquerading what lies beneath

Her smile.

INFOMERCIAL

Are you tired of taking care of others?
Did you grow up babysitting and hearing, take care of your brother or
sister?
Yes? Can be exhausting right?

Well, babysit yourself down!
Do I have the answer for you, the new Benevolent Balm
This product will NOT make you want to
help others, no,
it is a SYSTEM that has been created to
allow the wearer of this egocentric ointment to take care of themselves.

The administration of this cream is so
easy, it is virtually hands free
Yes, this self-care system is a colorless,
odorless saving salve that works much like oxyclean making
whites even whiter

Wow, amazing right? Wait, there's more!
This privilege preservation pack comes
with a tube of subjective serum, and for a limited time you are
also ENTITLED
to a revolutionary
Well maybe not revolutionary
But a reserved reflection of
responsibility tool.
Yes, this two way mirror has been crafted
to let you only appear to look at yourself.

With your purchase, for free, you also get
the new and improved, super night narcissistic nurturing wash
where at night you
don't have to be responsible for yourself at all.

Also if you call within the next fifteen minutes we will include not one, not two, but three vials of authentic 100% white girl tears.

Just a quick dab and you are insured
inclination
Perfect for the office, restaurants, banks
Just a few drops!
Ideal for holidays, grocery stores,
relationships and sidewalks
Imagine the surprise when a situation is
heading downhill, and magically you get a job, the blame is placed on someone
else, or people actually think you give a fuck
Not even Sham-Wow can soak these things
up! White girl tears are practically concentrated care.

The balm, the reflection, the tears, All
of this for just $19.95
This is made even easier when you combine
this offer with optional cry starter scripts purchased separately.
Examples are
A.
I'm
sorry, I just need to take a moment...
B.
Wait,
so this is my fault? Or...
C.
My
personal favorite...Oh my God, I'm just trying to help...

Other bundles include a white friend that
will validate all of the imaginary issues and first world problems you can
think of. This magic bullet of a product was formulated in Ferguson, Missouri
and has patented technology to fortify privilege.

37

Actually,, it targets other people to be the problem. Much like Proactive you won't have to deal with breakouts because you won't get locked up. Talk about George Foreman nonstick.

It gives you the freedom to walk across
the street without looking, to make connections without networking... to... fuck the
list, it just gives freedom

This product is all natural and won't leave an oily film. It also won't leave your skin orange, pink or any other color. The sticker is right on the front. Exclusively for white!

This product, may or may not be endorsed by the City of Austin, and has a full coverage Snuggie lifetime guarantee. You will have the
illusion that America is no longer taking care of you and you are doing it for
yourself.

Order now! Call 1-800-Go-White, that's 1-800-Go-White

Remember, some people are born with
privilege, others have to buy it, thank God for Benevolent Balm

No white girls were actually harmed during this advertisement.

Doc

JACKIE ROBINSON

A suicide lead off third...he's going for home! Robinson steals
home! Jackie Robinson steals home! He was Joe Louis in a ball
cap. With the dirt crunching beneath his cleats that was his
theme music. You couldn't satchel his pages. Faceless images
of defenders pounding their fists into pressed palms (both of us
pounding fist into gloves). Maybe he was afraid. the rooted
summers would grant no mercies at home. Plated by the
grinding threat that he didn't belong there.

So he runs.
You can hear his clothes whipping in the innocence of the wind.
So he runs.
It sounded like they were clapping. Praising
the galloping gambit through a gauntlet.
Wearing out his tennis shoes
like his welcome
going back and forth
every time the game set the match ablaze.

They relished
when he was in a pickle.
Escaping traps that sent Houdini to his grave.

Heavy handed retaliation whenever they thought he was being
a little too Sinatra to be frank about it.
They placed him in the same position as his class,
second,
and he received less chances than that.

A black face drowning in a sea of white ones...blazing for these
Brooklyn bums. With a shotgun and a map to Canada in his
back pocket
he takes off for third.

Legs churning like the butter at big mama's as a child, he
remembers.
39

The instant the rude moment slows he sees the children fixing their attention beneath the stands between the forest of ankles and legs, believing not what they see only empathizing with the (PRICE OF THIS FREEDOM) feeling.

Wondering if his life was more dangerous on the field or trying to get a room in the state of Mississippi. Wondering if life was more dangerous trying to steal a plate on the field or field a plate in the state of Mississippi.

Either way: It's a catch 42.

He was birthed by the bricks; he was built by the stones that the builder refused. Standing up in a puff of dancing dust, wiping off the dirt like death threats but damn. How many bags does a man have to steal before he finds his home base?

And apparently, serving your country doesn't get you served in this country, but I digress.

Robinson stands a few feet from third, exhausted from the spurs being cast from the stands. Robinson is eyeing the pitcher his final destination tickling his fancy. He inches closer to home base, the pitcher eyes him as he begins his windup So with a borrowed breath and hope soaking in his shoes, he runs! He's going for home, Robinson for our sons being broken and thrown to the bedrock; he runs. Robinson steals home with the ebon essence of fate driving him to the plate; he runs. Jackie Robinson steals home knowing he may be a Brooklyn bum, dodging the intersection of calloused mercies so those children buttoned beneath the stands can find their hope. **He's SAFE!** I can't believe what I just saw! Jackie Robinson steals home, oh my goodness!!

Scott Free

MAN UP

Sometimes I go to wine bars and see men order beer,
and, after I wonder why they're at a wine bar to begin
with, I wonder if they're just doing it to emasculate all the
prissy, wine-drinkin' nancy boys in the bar, like me. To
which I say "Man up, tough guy! Have a glass of wine!
Stop living under the shadow of what a man is supposed
to be and start living in the Sun of who you want to be."

...

When I travel the roadmap of my history of my becoming
a man, the bumps in the path are painful pinpricks in my
memory. If you cast those needle-point holes in my heart
against a black canvas,
you will see a constellation of contradiction,
each star a humiliation,
and when you connect the dots with enough imagination,
they outline the shape of what a man is supposed to be.
The true North Star is my father.
That dot there is the first time I got cut from a team,
there deciding to change my hallway commute to avoid a
bully
there the first time I, like my friends, mimicked the noises
of a retard, knowing full-well I was imitating my mother's
brother
there my first kiss, with a girl who was so into me, it
rivaled how much I was into the idea of kissing any girl at
all it didn't matter who
there the first time I was slapped in the face in gym class,
immediately followed by the first time I turned away to
Krazy-Glue my tear ducts,
because boys don't cry.

But boys who don't cry grow up to become men who
don't feel

41

and if the only emotions you allow
yourself to engage

are lust and aggression
then your world is small and cowardly.

Me being me involved a lot of lost chances.
And there's a point where you swallow your pride so
much,
you're swallowing the man you could've been.
And I am not the man I should've been. And neither are
you.

I've stood next to men,
men who put notches in belts and bedposts and souls,
who refused to apologize, because the cardinal sin of
Pride was more palatable than admitting a wrong,
because in error there is vulnerability, and men are not
vulnerable.
There are girls I should apologize to for not doing enough
and girls I should apologize to for doing too much.
Masculinity isn't in the area in-between, it's in
recognizing the faults in the extremes.
And there are boys I should apologize to whom I've
stepped on to get ahead, when finding a smaller boy was
a chance to prove I could learn from being dominated and
pass it down the food chain, because there is a
contagious language of violence among men accented by
humiliation.
Those that speak loudest elevate themselves to Alpha
poets.
Daily, I think about every swing and a miss, whether it's
baseball or beatdowns,
because every turned cheek was an opportunity to lose a
fight I could have bragged about later,
a chance for scars full of stories.

And I think about all the stupid shit I've done and all the

42

stupid shit I do and I wonder

"Is this what a real man does?"

But I am a man and, therefore,
everything I do
is what a real man does.

Michael Whalen

MAYAN PRIEST

A can full of soda. Coal. A pane of glass.
You
The behavior of the first three under pressure can be predicted.
But the fourth?
I would win at roulette five times before I could tell if ever I
touched your spirit.
17 black
It's obvious I lack the necessary gifts in this life to tell a smile
From a stab in the back
Or a kiss on the cheek from turning me over to a mob of
overzealous zealots.
In a garden at midnight.
Perhaps in the next life I will figure it out.
Rose petals. Words. Your picture.
All three affect me when pressed between pages.
The first reminds me. The second makes me think. And the
third reminds me
That thinking is dangerous.
But that's me. I've always been one to test the depth of the
water by jumping in with both feet.
And when I did, I met you.
Just call me shallow.
I poured out of myself like a broken bag of marbles and
buckshot
shocked and shot out in all different directions.
And for five seconds I would swear that gravity didn't work.
Or maybe it did, because I always have one foot in the past and
one on a roller skate
and fate is something I could never control.
I spent 17 lifetimes exploring you.
I would run my fingers through your soul, breathe in your
silence, and gaze deeply into your yesterdays.
But I could never see all of you.
No matter what glasses I wore, you were always 2-D.
Determined and distant.

44

Why do so longs take so long? Where's the good in goodbye or fair in farewell?

Well, I don't know. It's as if the devil that you know is so much better than the one you don't know.

But is it?

The devil that knows my nickname. How I sleep. Why I cry.

And I guess that's why I have started to treat strangers a whole lot better.

But just to let you know. I closed the barn door of my heart after you ran out.

I set the barn on fire hoping that you might run back. In the end it didn't matter.

I have made more sacrifices than a Mayan priest, and that was not the least.

My pride has laid on that stone slab altar at least
17 black lifetimes.

Always the screaming. But when my self-confidence lay there on that slab.

Silent. Wide eyed. Questioning.

I hesitated.

Resolve dissolved and I put the dagger down.

And now my mind is full. It can hold no more truths. One truth goes in, one goes out.

And I'm afraid if I learn anything else about myself or anyone gives me the advice I need to hear,

I'll forget where I am.

My back against the wall. Staring at the fact that I will probably never see you again.

And now for at least the 18th time

I am standing in a garden at midnight. I have finished a sad and mournful prayer.

A mob is approaching.

And I'm waiting to be kissed.

Allen Small

THE MEDLEY

I'm moving on y'all from poems to prayer-oetry
Woke up feeling battered and worn because God laid his
hands on me
He told me to treat every day like a baptism, so this is a
neophyte that you see
And he gave me directions (scriptures) to navigate through a
life (road) laden with treachery

Hoping I make it to the other side after I right the wrongs I've
done to humanity
Didn't write this to pass judgment, not qualified, consider it
therapy for me
Not sure where the words come from, but the stage is often
their ultimate destiny
Striving to be better than I was the day before, live simpler, and
eradicate unnecessary complexities

So the Lord gave me a problem on which my tears rely
And He came to me in absentia and He asked me not to cry
Not a sole (soul) was injured and no one had yet died,
but my heart was mortally wounded
still He asked me not to cry

I loved you (Mum, Dad, Carmen, Mamie, José, Solomon, and
Moses) before I knew you, and you're with me for all time

Realizing nothing can come between us, yet muffling my silent
cries
There is no way for me to fathom this news that mortifies,
because He spoke without any volume and He asked me not to
cry

Amen

Written by Angie Hodge for her "InnerVisions"

NAME

Speaking of cookie cutter...
Stop apologizing for your name
The forced guilt or shame when someone can't pronounce it right
And out of frustration with no more ounce of umph to fight
You give in to pressure and shorten it
A mouthful to bite off becomes just a little bit
I hate to see society take away pride
The heritage and culture that have to hide
When a foreign tongue butchers something beautiful and without remorse says "I tried"
Now conform and give me something "normal"
Something more formal and dignified
Something like Jones or Smith
Because the American dream is a myth
Built on the nightmare of generations who had to wake up and deal with
No longer being a king or queen, but instead being viewed as obscene or an abomination
The foundation of our great nation still steals whatever it feels like taking
And in most cases it's too obvious to make you kowtow or defer by crossing the street
So dominance is established when you first meet
It is like some still walk around with an invisible hooded sheet
The reality is that our individuality is broken down piece by piece
A handshake symbolizing peace
Is actually an olive branch hidden with a poisoned dart
It aims for your heart...it seeps in, creeps in... sinking beneath your skin
It reaches so far back it's hard to recollect when it really did begin...
Maybe as a child on your first day of school
When the roll call left you grasping at which is to rule

47

What you hear at home versus what your teacher spoke aloud
With each mispronounced letter "our way is better"
It is a simple message that brainwashes the cautious and the unsuspecting alike
That is why each time I get on the mic I go by Steffany
No, not Bethany...It's Steffany

S T E F F A N Y
S tand up for
T true
E quality
F ight
F earlessly
A gainst
N ame
Y ielding

It is a war and an army is building
Each time I refuse to be someone's PHANIE or PHANY
I believe it is my own battle cry from the depths of my soul
That I will not stand idly by as you try and fit us in a box you can control
From the scantron to the census bubble
I will always be trouble
Small town schools, corporate jobs, customer service...just a host trying to make a reservation
Will never mistake my dedication to the eradication of a subtle systematic racism
Yes, subtle with a B...
because it is written there so plainly to see
Each time Maria becomes Mary
Abdul is really, Abdel, but he doesn't tell because he doesn't want to look like a fool
All of the SuWanChings that become Debbie Su
Ngozi is really NNguzi not with an O but a U
Each time I meet someone new and ask them to repeat it one more time and attempt to spell it out
Please don't doubt my sincerity...

48

The Pens Of NeoSoul Poetry Slam

I am just trying to commit it to my mind
I want to respect you as a whole...
not a half truth from the start

Steffany ??

THE OCTOPUS SOLUTION

The octopus genome is so foreign scientists consider it alien. So, why don't we hunt it down? Why are we not punishing it for its differences? Why aren't we patrolling and policing the oceans to keep ourselves safe from these spineless aquatic thugs?

They are experts in the art of camouflage like sacrificing beards and locks. Then dawning ties to lynch blend in with corporate America.

Exceptionally intelligent but can't pass information from one generation to the next, like a black Mother it kills itself, watching the nest.

But where is the father?
Like too many black men
black boys,
having children
they don't stick around,
'cause no one stuck around for them,
'cause no one stuck around for them.

What do they have suction cups for if not to stick around?
Maybe men had suction cups they'd be more willing to stick around.

Thank God for short life spans and weak community.

Community!

Walls!

Why aren't we building walls around these oceans?
What if they crawl out and steal all the jobs we don't want?

Just imagine, all those arms reaching out for assistance and entitlements. Next, they'll all want equal opportunity and justice.

We need to stop this venomous creature before it spits more black ink.

The octopus is a clear and present danger!

Stop wasting money, building schools to teach them!

We need more prisons!

ODE TO JOY

Teresa Johnson

The music of Johnny Cash can be charitably described as
"depressing."
In his song "Man in Black," Cash addressed the people
who asked why he always dressed in dark colors
and sang about upsetting things.
He said, "'Til we start to make a move to make a few things right,
you'll never see me wear a suit of white."

I sent my second book of poems to my grandma,
and she wrote me a note saying
she's worried I won't ever come out of my "dark place."
She doesn't know if I know that I'm loved.
She asked me to write a poem called "Ode to Joy"
to help me keep my chin up.

I don't know how to tell her that at first the book was longer.
I don't know how to tell her about the three poems that were cut.
The first is about watching an abandoned kitten die,
the second is the beginning of the end of my closest friendship,
and the third is a list of the situations in which it might be best to get
an abortion.
I don't know how to tell this to my very Catholic grandma.
I don't know how to tell her I'm considered one of the funny ones.

I don't know how to tell her that the last poem I wrote
was about my other grandmother's death,
and how I don't regret her passing,
not because she hurt me, because she didn't,
but because of how she hurt my father.

Johnny Cash's songs weren't all depressing because his life was
depressing.
He wrote about the pain of others.
In "The Legend of John Henry's Hammer,"
he praised working-class people of color to his primarily white
audience.

52

In "The Ballad of Ira Hayes,"
he called white America to account for its treatment of Native
Americans and Veterans.
He sang "Folsom Prison Blues,"
in prisons.
How could he sing about the world as it was
and have it come out sunshine and rainbows?

I am blessed to write in a community that airs its grievances.
I have learned,
and been called out,
and had to change,
and had to shut up and listen.
Seeing the injustice of the world will turn your suit gray,
but learning you're part of the problem will turn it black.
Wearing black is slimming.
It'll help you trim your ego enough to see the needs of those around
you.
You will mourn the slow death of your former self,
but praise the friends willing to play pallbearer
and help bury the rotten parts of you in the ground.

Cash had plenty of his own reasons to hurt.
You can find a lot of them in the song, "Hurt."
And a lot of them were guilt.
He knew the ways he'd hurt other people,
in ignorance or selfishness or privilege,
and it pained him.
How could he stand in front of a crowd as his true self
and wear the shining white of a saint?

When someone finally starts swallowing their medicine,
don't feel bad that their mouth is full of bitterness.
This is what getting better tastes like.
It feels like setting a broken bone right again.
It feels like the nagging itch of healing skin.
It feels like being queasy all day,
and then finally just throwing up
and getting it all out.

53

So this is my Ode to Joy.
An ode to waking up every morning with a reason to fight.
An ode to becoming stronger by helping hold up other people.
An ode to friends patient enough to keep feeding you medicine.
An ode to surviving the everyday strain of living and knowing how to talk about it.
An ode to grandmas who listen
and whose first thought is to make sure you know you're loved.

OPEN LETTER TO MY HUSBAND

IN THE BIBLE IT SAYS THAT GOD CREATED THE
HEAVENS AND ALL THE EARTH IN 6
DAYS,
BUT ON THE 7TH DAY...
HE RESTED.
HE,
ALL POWERFUL BEING AND CREATOR,
RESTED.
YOU SEE EVEN GOD GETS TIRED SOMETIMES.
SHED TEARS TO CREATE OUR OCEAN,
WIPED THE SWEAT FROM HIS BROW TO GIVES US
RAIN.
SPLIT HIS SOUL IN 2 JUST TO GIVE US THE AIR WE
BREATHE...
YOU CAN'T TELL ME THAT'S NOT EXHAUSTING.
MY DEAREST HUSBAND,
NEED I REMIND YOU THAT THE STORY ALSO GOES
THAT WE WERE CREATED IN HIS
IMAGE?
THERE IS NOT A DOUBT IN MY MIND THAT WHEN YOU
LOOK AT ME YOU DON'T SEE
GOD.
JUST LIKE I HOPE YOU KNOW THAT WHEN I LOOK AT
YOU I SEE THE HEAVENS, AND ALL
THE EARTH.
MY ALPHA AND OMEGA.
BUT WHY MUST I REMIND YOU,
EVEN GOD GETS TIRED SOMETIMES.
IF EVEN HE, NEEDED A MOMENT OF REST AFTER
SHOULDERING THE WEIGHT OF THE
WORLD

55

THEN WHY NOT ME?
DO YOU NOT CONSIDER ME DESERVING?
WHEN THE WORLD LOOKS AND SEES THE MAGIC IN
MY SKIN,
IT EXPECTS ME TO BE ABLE TO PERFORM MIRACLES.
SHED MY TEARS TO QUENCH THE THIRST OF MY
CHILDREN SHOULD THEY EVER
NEED IT,
WIPE THE SWEAT FROM MY BROW TO RINSE THE
WORLD CLEAN.
SPLIT MY SOUL IN 2 JUST TO SACRIFICE ENOUGH FOR
MY DREAMS TO BREATHE.
AND ALL THE WHILE THEY STAND ADMIRING MY
STRENGTH FOR ITS BEAUTY,
BUT IN THE SAME BREATH DEMONIZING ME FOR
USING IT.
I KNOW MY WORTH, AFTER ALL I DO CONSIDER
MYSELF WORTHY OF YOU.
I LOVE ME, JUST AS MUCH AS I LOVE YOU.
AND THERE IS NOT A FORCE ON THIS EARTH
THAT CAN MAKE ME QUESTION THE DEFINITION I
HAVE WRITTEN FOR MYSELF.
EXCEPT YOU.
YOU ARE MY SEVENTH DAY.
MY SAVING GRACE,
MY "YOU'VE DONE GOOD, AND IT'S OK TO REST NOW."
YOUR ARMS BE MY SANCTUARY, MY GARDEN OF EDEN.
SO WHEN I AM TIRED OF SHOULDERING THE WEIGHT
OF THE WORLD
PLEASE DO NOT CHASTISE ME FOR BEING HOMESICK.
WHEN I COME TO YOU TO BREAK, I KNOW THAT EVERY
OUNCE OF LOVE FOR ME IN YOU
WILL WANT TO FIX ME.
AND SOMETIMES THAT WILL BE OK.

BUT MOST OF THE TIME....
ALL I WILL NEED YOU TO DO IS CATCH THE PIECES.
HOLD THEM TIGHT, AND CLOSE.
KISS THEM GENTLY AND STROKE THEIR HAIR.
AND WHEN THEY ARE FINALLY DONE FALLING...
JUST HAND ME THE GLUE.
THOUGH I CONSIDER MYSELF EXCEPTIONAL,
WORTH MY WEIGHT IN GOLD AND THEN SOME.
THE WEIGHT ON THESE SHOULDERS GETS HEAVY.
THE SIGMAS, THE RUMORS, THE STEREOTYPE, AND
DIRTY LOOKS BE HEAVY,
AND I AM NO ATLAS OR IMMORTAL WARRIOR.
I AM ONLY HUMAN.
I KNOW THAT IRON SHARPENS IRON
BUT EVEN THE BEST OF SWORDS NEED TO BE COOLED
AFTER SO MUCH FRICTION
SO WHEN I COME TO YOU,
STRIPPED OF MY ARMOR AND VULNERABLE,
I NEED YOU TO UNDERSTAND THAT THIS IS THE MOST
INTIMATE PART OF ME THAT I CAN
GIVE.
SO I WILL ASK YOU PLEASE,
TRY YOUR BEST TO REMEMBER THAT EVEN GOD GETS
TIRED...
SOMETIMES.

~Shanitra Harris

SEMICOLON

For Charlotte,
Who Had to Take her Dog to the Emergency Vet Again Today

I can't take a broken thing and make it run.
I can't put glass pieces back into a window
and keep the baseball on the other side forever.
I can't do trigonometry, or calculus, or long division.

I can't solve for any of the unknowns
in my life:
I can't make no money plus no money
add up to rent.
I can't make money plus effort add up
to decent, home cooked meal,
I can't make empty apartment plus empty hand divided by
empty bed
equal up to love.

I can barely remember to buy the fancy cat food
I like to buy for my cat.

I spend a lot of time crying. Leaking.

In the winter, when it rains, I am a house
with a busted pipe—I am not flooding
because of the storm, but because
something inside me, something a part of me
broke just in time to have me blaming someone else.

I can't fix your problems.
I can't even fix my own.

But I like to think I can help.
That listening without trying to solve
your life like an algebra problem

is the best gift I can give you.
Like maybe that's what I'm here for,
I am not a tool box or a sewing kit,
but instead a jar: shatterable, fragile,
but made for holding.

Maybe that's the only reason I am still alive:
To be a container for things no one else can hold.

Maybe the reason the semi-colon became the symbol
for resisting suicide is not merely
that you keep on going when you could have stopped
but that you keep on going
because you are connected to the things around you.

I am thankful,
not that you are hurting, but that you trust
me with your pain.

Maybe that's the dream: not to live free of pain
but to live in pain, safe in the knowledge
that you will be cared for.

On the day I almost died on purpose
the worst part was not the pain.
Despair is survivable.

The worst part wasn't the melancholy,
not the tears,
not the panic attack,
not the certainty that life would never be better—
Depression is survivable.

The worst part was that when I picked up the phone,
There was no one I wanted to call.

Dejection, Displeasure, Deprivation
all are survivable.

59

Austin NeoSoul

But—
disconnection is the deadliest foe I have ever met.

So I can't give your dog stitches
or lower your rent
or repair whatever is wrong with your car,
I don't sweat superglue,
Basically, I can't fix shit.

But if you need somewhere to whisper your pain,
I can cup my hands around your truth.

We all walk these roads carrying lumpy burdens
hard to get a grip on,
Maybe I am still alive today to be
an extra pair of hands.

Maybe holding up the people around me
is how I become strong enough
to carry myself.

Glori B

SING TO ME

By Kelenne Blake-Fallon

Breaking chains like
Bob
Fela
Breaking barriers like
Billy
Etta
Breaking stereotypes
Jimi
Nina
Breaking...
Michael
Whitney
Countless others
ignited by shrill brass
and lyrical mettle
All music is political
So tell me
Star
what kind of party are you playing for
When that beat flows through streets
will it make the people move
or will it move the people
Do you even know your power
Star
How do your fingers dance on strings
while another mother frets
about another son detained
Promote cars, clothes and coitus
to capitalism's consumers
or sing for children dying of consumption
for debt slaves for whom death is a promotion
sing for barefoot sweatshop laborers
making shoes they could never buy
or sing to uphold status quo

61

are you just white noise
or will you make some noise
Sing to me
Baby
I want to hear that rebel music
unlock my mind with the keys you hit
Play me an anti-lullaby
wake me up
make me move
unfetter my restless feet
merge your baseline with my heartbeat
check the pulse in my unchecked wrists
as I pound the air with my clenched fist
blast bass
rattle my ribcage
my consciousness
make my blood boil on the fire
pouring from your saxophone
Baby
can you set me ablaze
Then
and only then
will I sing along
will I dance barefoot on hot coals
will I gladly traverse
all seven circles of your hell
if that's what it takes
to give birth to the
harmony trapped in your
rhapsody
Baby
sing to me

STRONGER THINGS

Tell yourself you can't.
Tell yourself not today
Say you aren't able
you can't afford it
it's not the right time
you're not strong enough
no one else wants to
it's just you
it's too hot
it's too cold
you're tired
you don't feel right
it doesn't feel right
they'll say no
they'll say yes
you'll fail
and they'll all laugh
they'll all laugh
and you'll die
you'll die right there, so
tell yourself any excuse to
avoid
or
evade
cite every drawback
cop out
tell yourself anything
to help you believe
you should do
nothing
and say it
loud enough...
...for me to hear you.
So I can call you a liar to your face.
So I can grab you by your neck

63

pull you out of the
mire
the muck and mud of your self-pity
and douse you with the water of what I believe
because
I believe you should end.
I believe you should die.
I believe your life should cease
so you can live the life you held on back order
like the shoe that actually fit
You're not allergic to the light baby
you just don't want it on you and I don't get it
because that is all I see come out of you
when your arms aren't folded.
Acknowledge that you even have arms
quit complaining you don't have the strength
because if that was the truth
you wouldn't hold on to things like you do.
You are not a prisoner
you are a warden in a one person prison
and what's worse
you're a workaholic
wreak havoc
on your hopelessness
subtract it from the whole of you
believe less in your doubts
you cannot say that life is pointless
if you won't pick your head up
and look where it's pointing you
scream 'I love you' in a crowd loud enough for you to
hear it
and revel in the nervous happiness; it's
called glowing.
You are everything
you wish you were
you just don't wish to realize it
pass on the plates of opinion
unless

they can feed you
and you not suffer the indigestion of indecision
turn 'why didn't I' into 'why didn't I do sooner'
change 'I don't know' from question
to statement
quit whining
unless you're trying to make someone laugh
thereby making yourself a superhero
accept your own friend request
quit fighting with yourself unless you're just sparring
for when you need to get it on with anyone trying to
knock you off
I'm not saying look for a fight
just don't run from it;
pretending it's not there doesn't mean it will play
along.
Be the devil unto your demons
just because you created them
don't mean they get an easy ride
File a restraining order on your self restraint
and be the devil
unto your demons
just because you created them doesn't mean they
get a free ride
quit reading motivational posters we both know
you
don't
listen,
hell
you're probably not even paying attention to this
poem.
It's called
life;
and it happens.
And yes baby
you
have to act like you want it
but it is not yours.

65

Austin NeoSoul

It is a path.
It twists and it turns
and you have to go where it goes
and if you walk it just right
you get to rest while those not as far as you ask you for the
directions
and should you reach the end
there is only everything waiting for you
with the honor of a memory
you
are so much more than misery
but it is not up to me to be you
just be grateful I know you
I am always
standing there with you, behind you
and just in front of you
above you with all those who love you
waiting for you
to erupt from that thick husk
cut through the callous of
your condition and call whatever comes out your
character
to finally accept a truth
you won't hear
as you adhere to your cherished fears;
that we are a
ma
zing.
That we are made of both his and each other's love.
That we are both fearfully & wonderfully made.
That
we

are made of stronger things!

Joe B

The Pens Of NeoSoul Poetry Slam

TEXAS TEA

$1.79 for gas.

That is so cheap I want to pour it all over my body,
slather it on like sunscreen.
I think I want to swim in gasoline.

I'm gonna fill up my electric car.
I'm gonna fill the frame of my bicycle.
(Doesn't that make it heavier?)
Yeah, but it's so cheap...
I wanna start using it as a condiment.
Slap it on my sandwich like mayonnaise...
I wanna use it as a glaze on my Easter ham!
Gol'damn!
That's so cheap I wanna start drinking it!
Move over Long Island Iced Tea!
gimme some Texas Tea!
Hoowee!
That's cheaper than a one liter bottle of Ozarka water at the
same station!

I'm used to only seeing this number grow!
Holy frak! How did it get so low?

Well holy frak, they fracked the holes.
(What does that mean?)
It's not that complicated.

Here in America, we had all this oil we couldn't get to with drills
because it was too deep underground.

So we've been using this new technique called "hydraulic
fracturing" or "fracking,"
which is where they take clean water,
and mix it with toxic chemicals,

67

Austin NeoSoul

and then pump it into the oil wells,
and it forces the oil out!

They leave most of the toxic stuff underground to contaminate
the drinking water and soil,
but that doesn't matter 'cause now we've got all this oil!

Just… so much oil.
I'm gonna use it to deep fry my turkey this year.
So much oil we're gonna need America's whole breadbasket to
sop it up.

So anyways, OPEC,
            (the Organization of Petroleum Exporting Countries!)
Right. They control most of the world's oil production,
            (which means they generally control the price of oil!)
Right. They saw that America had all this oil,
so they're maintaining high production,
which is artificially reducing the price of oil.

And that's why a gallon of gas suddenly costs the same as a
grande coffee from Starbucks,
or half a tall mocha from Starbucks,
or a third of a bag of ground roast beans from Starbucks.
I'm just saying,
Starbucks coffee is unreasonably expensive.
Yet oil is surprisingly cheap right now!

Cheaper than a used Dave Matthews CD.
Cheaper than a joke about Dave Matthews.
            (He's actually pretty good.)

I agree. You know what's not good?
We didn't used to have earthquakes in Texas.
We started fracking around in Dallas.
Now,
earthquakes in Dallas,
every year since.

68

The Pens Of NeoSoul Poetry Slam

What's not good is oil barons stealing back the shitty land we
gave the Native Americans in the Dakotas,
so they can profit from poisoning it.

What's not good is flammable tap water in homes too close to
fracking sites.
Thousands of Americans with cancer from living to close to
fracking sites.

Anyways, fracking is where you take clean water and trade it for
cheap gas.

And now you can buy gas for less than a gallon of water at that
same station.

VIBIN

We were vibin'
You know-Like Dizzie and Ella,
Just finding our strings
And notes
And
The light shined through our conversation
And it had us feeling so full
I mean-
we were ego trippin with Nikki
while we soaked our souls in
                Gwendolyn's brooks

He felt me ----Ya know?
And without warning
And we fell
into the humming frequency
of Cole's train and he made
                my tracks
                        and my
voyage was so fantastic
and he told me to come and ride
and ride
and ride
and we did
for Miles and miles and through Muddy Waters
and cloudy skies

We spent our Pennies from Heaven to sip that tea
To read our leaves
That would tell us of centuries of connections unbroken

Together we left our prints in Dust Tracks on a Dirt Road
While our Eyes Were Watching God
We bumped into Billie who fed us her Strange Fruit
We felt the pain her soul as she sang us her deepest of
blues...

We ran into a Monk, Thelonious's melodious hideaway what
we needed to regroup

We climbed Crystal Stairs that glimmered with Hughes so
brightly
We became Invisible Man

We traveled to the land of Native Son,
He told us, Things-Things Fall Apart
Gave us wisdom, reminded us to remember our ancestors,
Where we came from,
Taught us how to go back, where to start

So we returned in God's Traveling Shoes,
A day late and a dollar short

That afternoon we met coffee,
Bebe said "Your Blues Ain't Like Mine"
Sula cried as she explained she felt violated by The Bluest
Eye
We saw her broken wings, wanted them to mend so she could
fly...

That vibe,
The vibe reluctantly brought us home
and though sad, it was unforgettable

71

Austin NeoSoul

But it assured us
It was just resting
Cause see it's there
The vibe-
Is the movement,
Voice,
Space
And place
Where we as artists
Are ALWAYS free.

©Sarah J. Uphoff (2004)

The Pens Of NeoSoul Poetry Slam

WE USED TO BE KINGS

16 years ago we were all kings.
Conquering corner store daydreams
and ice cream trucks.
Before tag became a blood sport,
before hopscotch meant avoiding-
stepping over chalk outlines of
those who became hieroglyphs-
before we became good at
reading hieroglyphs, we were all innocent.

We learned how to clutch onto it,
grip it with greasy fingers
after eating las quesadillas de mi Madre
as if to never let go.

Although our neighborhood was the
type of place where cliques and kodak moments
never clicked together, we still knew
how to smile, find our happiness in an ugly place,
pose for a picture worth a thousand platinum
hip hop records.
We knew we could be gone the next snapshot-
become as disposable as the camera that
shot our smiles one by one-
become as disposable as the camera that
framed our picture at a high-end art gallery
without knowing we were royalty.

Every person, every face, every place
was a postcard, pitch perfectly screaming-
wish you make it out.

My parents still hold stacks of stamps,
with dried out tongues and sore arms
of gently putting postcards under my pillow
trying not disturb the only time I didn't
have to live in a ghetto.

73

Postcards of six little kings, claiming our
kingdom on the top of Southport Drive.
But there were too many conquistadores
trying to reclaim our kingdom.
Too many blue bonnets and red roses
being handed out in exchange for early spring funerals.
Every year after,
the gardens didn't bloom as much.
The bouquets of chrysanthemums and lilies
couldn't hold together much longer.
Our picture frames got smaller.
The coffins grew larger.
Our numbers decreased, as we kept dying-
our memories deceased, as our mothers
kept crying.
Our fathers defeated from building our
coffins.
The photographer couldn't sell out anymore,
she said Sunday funerals didn't make
good business.

But every year after,
I still posed.
I still smiled.
I managed to follow my happiness
out of an ugly place.
But most importantly, I still go back.
Hoping to still find our chip-toothed
smiles and Saturday morning cartoons.
Hoping to still find our innocence.
Hoping to find my friends and pose
for a better tomorrow--
but the reality is I don't know
where most of them are now a days_or
how many have passed away.

Julian Copaldo

YOKAMI MITSU WANTS TO DIE

a poem by John Crow

Monday morning meeting, you started speaking, I checked out. I mean really I stopped listening to you after the second vowel. The very sound of your voice causes me an ear infection that drips down my throat making me cough out phlegm bubbles of fuck you under my breath.

The others know I checked out also and try to invite my attention back to the conversation that only you are having with them because I'm not there anymore.

The rub is I fought to be here. Where my very presence is always a question of intense stares and bewildered looks. Who is he? What is he? Why is he here? How come the boss knows him? All valid questions that I answer with my own F-you blank expression.

The kind of look that says I'll eat the watermelon on the fruit tray and not cover it up. But what I am covering up is my growing need to make this guy with a voice that sounds like Lou Rawls and Adele, stuffed themselves into a chicken, who is trying to talk from inside Gilbert Godfrey's vagina to shut the hell up.

It's amazing how much of the air in the room diminishes every time you inhale

I am looking at the plant in the corner, it's a Japanese Ficus.

It's sending me a message I see the words kill him spelled out in the dead leaves at the bottom of its pot. I nod to the plant and it could be the air-conditioning the plant nods back.

Nature hates the sound of your voice to. All living things other than bacteria and maggots want you to stop making those strange noises with your mouth.

The sound is offensive to everything but flies... I'm wrong flies hate it too I just saw one land on the Ficus.

Every time we take a meeting we bring our baggage with us. We swap stories and we swap lives. My luggage fits into a small carry-on... Why do you keep... No hoard so much shit...

Let go... They go an app for that...

Let go and let God. They go a church for that.

Won't he do it?

Won't he will?

Will he won't make you please stop talking.

I wonder how someone could miss the fact that I stopped listening for anything other than the buzz words that should trigger a response from me but does not... I am even unaware that you called me by name. How far gone do you have to be not to notice that if I am not responding to my name... I am not responding to you

The leaves on the Ficus, who calls herself Yokami Mitsu, uses her leaves to point to a garbage can as if to say: either make you stop talking or put her in it. She is here at every meeting and has decided to commit seppuku but she is rooted to that spot, and needs my help to end her suffering.

I notice the office garbage can is just big enough for your head. Yokami wonders why I don't do something... how long can I keep **not** doing something.

Thank you for giving me a printed copy of every one of your 75 PowerPoint slides. Complete with notes and commentary... Yet you feel the need to go through each one... As if I can't read. You may as well have called me ignorant. OH hell NO! My face wears that serene smile I've practiced.

I even nod to make it look like I'm not looking at how many witnesses will have to be found.. in the past tense... like those folks who were going to testify in Flint.

YoKami laughs the way only a plant that wants to die can laugh. She uses one of her many branches to mock me. She says unless someone dies no one will care. How true. We said bring back our girls and they took more.

We said occupy Wall Street, and it got gentrified.

We said say no to drugs.

We said stop the violence.

We said no to genetically altering our food

We said no supporting black business on black Friday. That worked.

We keep saying our lives matter... she asks, "how is that going?" She gives me the Ficus version of the finger.

But I am rooted to this spot just as you are Yokami.. I can't shake the dirt that's holding me down.

A little shit makes you stronger... For me shit just gets repeated. This shit isn't new, it just gets repeated, remixed, recycled, we keep recycling the shit that holds us back.

It's time for a break..the slide says so

I get up

Excuse myself to the bathroom

Dump my coffee into Yokami Mitsu's pot.

I tell her "See you next Monday."

And walk to my office not looking back.

77

YOU

My pen loves to write you
The way words dance off your tongue
The waltz when you woo me
The close and slow when you console me
A little BBoy when you talk about your passions and
A jitterbug when you celebrate
My pen moves to write you
You
The way you walk
Rhythmic and intentional
Fashion unconventional
Unique, but professional
You
Have a sparkle in your eye when you get a new idea
Tear up when you see pain and suffering
You see right through facades
Invading other people's boxes of secrets by accident with
nothing but a glance
Deconstructing their delusions of grandeur with one constriction
of your iris
My pen sees you
You
Are intelligent and empathetic
Quickly bored with pedestrian rhetoric
Hungry for knowledge with a
Thirst that can only be quenched by truth
My pen loves to drink you
You
Shine a little too bright
Burn a little too hot
Most people don't know if they can handle you or not, but
You
Walk in your truth anyway
Unapologetically
The only way you know how to be
The only view you can see

Above these clouds

Chasing your dreams with
Passion pulling you apart at the seams into
Pieces of you
Y
O
U
Walking this earth and reading these stars putting pieces
together
Star maps and moonlit paths the inky guide you need

You...
I hated that all my pen could talk about was you
Until I realized
This was all from my pen's first person point of view and
The you my pen meant wasn't you at all
It was me
My pen sees in the dark and
Sees my darkness and still
All my pen can do is shine a light on the masterpiece that is
Me
My pen loves to write you
You
Me
I was so busy worrying about you
I forgot about me and
My pen was reminding me the whole time
My pen loves to write you and
Reminded me I'm a you too
My pen moves to write you
My pen sees me
In pieces of you
M
E
Pick up your pieces...

Sunni Soper

79

Angie – (Aun Gee)

She's British

Jomar Valentin

How long have you been writing/performing poetry?

I began writing poetry in 3rd grade. I actually won a national award for young writers when my family and I still lived in the Philippines. One of my teachers submitted my work without telling me so the award was a huge surprise! I began performing in 2008.

How would you describe your style of poetry?

I would say that each of my poems are like elaborate answers to possible interview questions about myself.

What is your favorite thing about poetry?

My favorite thing about poetry is the storytelling aspect that comes with it.

Tell us about your first time reading at Neo and do you remember what poem you read (if so what was the name)?

I was introduced to NeoSoul in 2009 when it was held at Club Illusions. I read a poem called "I Will Build You A City."

Danny "DNY" Strack

How long have you been writing/performing poetry?

I've been writing poetry since high school (about 20 years) and performing for 13 years.

How would you describe your style of poetry?

I'd describe my style of poetry as systematic, obfuscated, highfalutin, word-play-oriented, and attempting to be comedic.

What is your favorite thing about poetry?

I love how open poetry is to interpretation. I love how it sounds when spoken.

Tell us about your first time reading at Neo and do you remember what poem you read (if so what was the name)?

I don't remember what poem I read the first time I came to NeoSoul, but I think it was either "Chalk" or "Cloud Carnival of Cairo." I remember everyone being very nice...but I'm not sure if they were impressed by the poems or not. I think it was out in Pflugerville (the first time we were out there). Find me at www.dannystrack.com!

Kim "13"

How long have you been writing/performing poetry?

I started writing in the 9th grade, Miss Coulter's English.

How would you describe your style of poetry?

I do not consider myself a poet. I am a writer.

What is your favorite thing about poetry?

Expression and truth in its purest form.

Tell us about your first time reading at Neo and do you remember what poem you read (if so what was the name)?

I read "Sundays In Harlem." I guess it was Neo's 3rd home, "Skinny Sahara". Maybe 2004/2005ish? Brian did a poem for our Agency's Black History Program. He was good friends with my Deputy Director. My friend Nicole fell in love with him, as did most of the women in our office!!! He talked to a few of us and told us about Neo. Nicole knew I was a writer, so we came up with a plan to attend. My voice cracked and shook as I struggled to get through the poem. I traveled extensively during the first year, so I was not there every week, but I met up with Ron, Brian and KA on Yora for writing labs, chicken and poet wine. Lol, Brian's brother Tweety would critique and cook. Those were the best times. We didn't write and recite for applause and scores; it was an extension of our hearts, community and souls.

Sarah "Cousin Sarah"

How long have you been writing/performing poetry?

I have written poetry since I was in the 5th or 6th grade. I often wrote because it gave me a safe space to express whatever I was feeling without having to censor myself. It gave me the right to have a voice. It would often be how I worked to heal emotional wounds. Or imagine new possibilities. I believe it gave me confidence, a place I could be my full self.

How would you describe your style of poetry?

I wouldn't say my poetry has a style. If I had to pick a term, I would say authentic storytelling. Sometimes that story may be to heal a wound. Or make change. Or share something of value to me. Or to play with the beauty of language.

What is your favorite thing about poetry?

I have always loved clever word play-from Hip Hop to authors like Lewis Carroll. Each story is a part of me in someway.

Tell us about your first time reading at Neo and do you remember what poem you read (if so what was the name)?

First time I read at Neo was in 2004. I didn't even know there was such a thing as people reading poetry out loud to others aka Spoken Word. LaLove was the host and she was joking with the audience and it felt like a home. You could feel the community almost instantly. BFran walked up to us before we even got to a table, introduced himself and said "We hug here. Welcome to Neo, we're so glad to have you." I sat down and watched poet after poet bring me to laughter and tears. I wrote a poem on the back of one of their flyers. I kept debating if I had the nerve to go up and read and my friend encouraged me, so I finally did. I was so nervous and kept thinking I'm soooo out of my league. As I was reading people kept snapping and clapping in support. When I finished 13 yelled from the back of the venue "THAT'S MY COUSIN!!!" And I've been Cousin Sarah ever since. I went to Neo almost every week for well over 5 years. Even in times where life has kept me away more, Neo was always one of the most incredible examples of community I've experienced in this lifetime. Spoken Word and Neo impacted and changed my life significantly. My PhD research has been around Spoken Word and adult learners, what poetry can teach us. Without my experiences at Neo, those fruits would have never come to fruition. I'm grateful for it.

LaLove Robinson

How long have you been writing/performing poetry?

I've been writing since 2nd grade. Performing for 15 years.

How would you describe your style of poetry?

My style is colorful, blunt and personal.

What is your favorite thing about poetry?

My favorite thing about poetry is the therapy.

Tell us about your first time reading at Neo and do you remember what poem you read (if so what was the name)?

My first time reading at NeoSoul was an audition at Major D's for NeoSoul Founder, Herman Mason and others. It was nerve racking. Herman thought I was too in your face, lol. The first poem I read was a poem about my dad titled, "Something To Say."

Jacob Dodson

How long have you been writing/performing poetry?

I've been doing performance poetry with some regularity since 2009. I was writing poetry before that as well, but it all sucked.

How would you describe your style of poetry?

My poetry style is largely comedic - it's the lens through which I often view things and how I feel like engaging with topics that are less funny.

What is your favorite thing about poetry?

My favorite thing about poetry is me performing it. Being in control of an audience and making them share a laugh is both exhilarating and affirming.

Tell us about your first time reading at Neo and do you remember what poem you read (if so what was the name)?

I'm not sure that I remember my first time reading at Neo. I think I remember the first time I went, it was a slam over at Club Illusions? (the one in Pflugerville) and there were 16 poets there so I didn't get to read that night. Then I came back at some point and read something apparently forgettable.

Lizz

How long have you been writing/performing poetry?

I've been writing since high school. Performing since 2006.

How would you describe your style of poetry?

My poetry style is real life relatable and story-form.

What is your favorite thing about poetry?

My favorite thing about poetry is the ability to put your feelings on paper and people can relate.

Tell us about your first time reading at Neo and do you remember what poem you read (if so what was the name)?

My first time reading at Neo was 2005. I can't recall my first piece, but it was off paper lol. I've done slam so I can't remember, that fried my brain.

ShelbyRae Holton

How long have you been writing/performing poetry?

I have been writing poetry since middle school, but performing since August of 2015.

How would you describe your style of poetry?

My poetry style is very raw and honest. I write a lot about things I have personally faced.

What is your favorite thing about poetry?

I love how it gives a voice to people who often feel unheard, how it heals and builds a beautiful community, and how it helps me to keep growing as a person.

Tell us about your first time reading at Neo and do you remember what poem you read (if so what was the name)?

My first time at Neo, I wondered why everyone was so touchy feely (HUGLIFE), but I felt very loved and

welcomed. I read a piece called "Numbers," which was the first time I ever vocally expressed I had an eating disorder. It was a very healing experience.

Brian "BFran" Francis

How long have you been writing/performing poetry?

I wish I could say all my life...about 14 years or so.

How would you describe your style of poetry?

I am passionate, musical, positive, and all about the cause of human trafficking and homelessness.

What is your favorite thing about poetry?

The truth of it, the passion, the many different ways to say the same thing.

Tell us about your first time reading at Neo and do you remember what poem you read (if so what was the name)?

I read the very first night of NeoSoul's existence...Major D's...oxtails, greens, chitlins. The name of the poem "You F&$king Hurt," with love to my wife...yea it was like that before the kind and sweet BFran.

Ebony Stewart

How long have you been writing/performing poetry?

I started writing poetry at age 8. Wackiest shit ever.

How would you describe your style of poetry?

Austin American-Statesman described my poetry as "beasty," but I'm a life writer. I write about my life, so it's honest and relatable.

What is your favorite thing about poetry?

I love the idea of freedom in poetry. The connections we make. I stay falling apart and putting myself back together in my poems.

Tell us about your first time reading at Neo and do you remember what poem you read (if so what was the name)?

First poem I read at Neo was "Microphone Fiend." Neo came and did a few nights in San Marcos downtown George's. I got to perform and hear LaLove (who I fell in love with). I was nervous and confident at the same time. Then Cousin Sarah took me to the OG Neo at Club Sahara's and I got to spit one mo' 'gin. Met 13, Angel, BFran, and Jo. Been family ever since. And forever will be.

Faylita Hicks

How long have you been writing/performing poetry?

I've been writing and performing poetry for 15 years.

How would you describe your style of poetry?

Surrealist.

What is your favorite thing about poetry?

It's ability to capture moments, tell stories and change lives in the fewest words.

Tell us about your first time reading at Neo and do you remember what poem you read (if so what was the name)?

I was a side kick, snuck in the building with Terry Collins. I didn't read until some time later, and by then, I had finally completed some sad poem about my life sucking. I don't remember. That's probably a good thing.

Robert "ScottFree"

How long have you been writing/performing poetry?

I've been writing poetry for 11 years.

How would you describe your style of poetry?

I've never written a non-fiction poem. My style is rough, hard, and in your face.

Tell us about your first time reading at Neo and do you remember what poem you read (if so what was the name)?

I met LaLove Robinson and Da'Shade Moonbeam at an open mic where they told me about NeoSoul. The first poem I did was called, "The GOAT." I bragged how I was the best poet ever, ironically, I was terrible at the time.

Mike Whalen

How long have you been writing/performing poetry?

I started performing poetry in 2004.

How would you describe your style of poetry?

I try to write funny, yet meaningful poetry.

What is your favorite thing about poetry?

I love the sense of community and the truly brilliant work.

Tell us about your first time reading at Neo and do you remember what poem you read (if so what was the name)?

When I was just starting to perform, I met LaLove Robinson at an open mic and she invited me to NeoSoul, which, at that time, was at the Historic Victory Grill. Brian Francis hosted that night and, before I read, I asked him if it was okay to curse. He then went back to the mic and said, "He just asked me if it was okay to curse. HELL YEAH, IT'S OKAY TO CURSE!" And then I read "The Triumph of Eugene Garkowsky," a poem ostensibly about bowling, which includes curse words. Twitter: @mikepwhalen

Allen Small

How long have you been writing/performing poetry?

I have written and performed poetry for almost 9 years.

What is your favorite thing about poetry?

I love the talent, commitment, and diversity of the poet community. I love the community. The poets are greater than the poetry and the poetry is phenomenal.

Tell us about your first time reading at Neo and do you remember what poem you read (if so what was the name)?

The first poem I ever did was called "Home Improvement Project," analyzing how a relationship is like a home.

Steffany Overby

How long have you been writing/performing poetry?

I have been writing all of my life...but I didn't actually start sharing my poetry until I attended my 1st ever open Mic at NeoSoul in 2006.

How would you describe your style of poetry?

Uhm...it rhymes. Lol I don't really have a set format...sometimes I feel a little HallMarkish compared to other poets because of the rhyming, but I never follow a guideline for topic or rhythm or length.

What is your favorite thing about poetry?

What I love about poetry...welp...everything. I have never Slammed, but I love the opportunity poetry gives me to make a real change and impact.

Tell us about your first time reading at Neo and do you remember what poem you read (if so what was the name)?

My 1st time at NeoSoul was back at Antonio's Tex Mex in 2006. While I was waiting for my turn, I asked the DJ how the poet got the stage name Element615 – the DJ aka NeoSoul Founder, Herman Mason - told me it was because Joe B.'s birthday was on June 15th...I was super excited and told him that was my birthday..and then Herman told me it was his birthday, too! NeoSoul has been family ever since. The poem I read was called "Race N Class." I was nervous...my hands trembled and my knees shook...but it is actually the only piece I have committed to memory to this day that I can recall to perform on the spot.

Christopher Michael

How long have you been writing/performing poetry?

I started slamming in 1999.

How would you describe your style of poetry?

I'm not sure. Maybe you should ask someone else. I try to be multi-faceted, funny, dramatic, and entertaining with the truth hidden inside.

What is your favorite thing about poetry?

I love that I'm good at it.

Tell us about your first time reading at Neo and do you remember what poem you read (if so what was the name)?

My first time at Neo was 2004. I went with my boy Mahess. I'm pretty sure my first poem was a group piece with him and we KILLED IT! The poem was called "Love & Hate." www.mrmichael310.com

Twitter/Instagram/Facebook: @mrmichael310.

Teresa Johnson

How long have you been writing/performing poetry?

My first poetry slam was on June 11, 2013 at Austin Poetry Slam. I did very badly, but kept coming back. Three years, three nationals teams, and two chapbooks later, it's still worth it to keep coming back.

How would you describe your style of poetry?
How would you describe your poetry style: I'm an argument poet: I write to make a point and persuade others to see their place in it. I use humor, satire, myth, storytelling, allegory, and personal experience to spin the yarn that wins hearts and minds over to the point I'm trying to make. There are lots of dragons and shouting and woman power and God and sea creatures and overblown southern accents and foot stomping and hopefully some laughter.

What is your favorite thing about poetry?

Poetry gives me something productive to do with my voice. I don't really have to worry about my voice not being heard: I have natural assertiveness on top of a lot of privilege. So if I'm going to take up space and write and perform and get heard, it can't be only for my own sake. Poetry channels my inborn confidence into methods that support and edify others. The slam community teaches me about the needs of others less fortunate than myself and the ways a person with privilege can be a useful ally. The slam format reminds me that I do deserve to be heard, but so does everyone else and speaking must always come with listening. The friends I've made in slam give me opportunities to practice love and kindness and gentleness and all the other things I'm not always good at when I'm too caught up in competition. To put it simply: poetry gives me direction.

Tell us about your first time reading at Neo and do you remember what poem you read (if so what was the name)?

I got on the mic the first time I went to Neo, at Quantum Lounge in 2013. I don't remember the poem I read, but I'll never forget what Brian Francis said to me afterward: "You don't know it yet, but Neo is your home." In my head, I was like, "okay, kind old man," and I didn't think too much of it. After all, I had gotten my start at APS, Neo seemed smaller, Quantum Lounge was a strangely-organized space... I didn't realize then

96

what Neo would mean to me. When I look back on it, I see now what I should have seen then: that Neo gives you what you give it, that everything worth having takes work, that even small communities produce powerhouse poets. Facebook: Teresa Johnson. Hit me up to buy chapbooks, get details on upcoming performances, and read a steady stream of feminist reposts.

Glori B

How long have you been writing/performing poetry?

4½ years

How would you describe your style of poetry?

I'd call my style confessional.

What is your favorite thing about poetry?

I love that poetry encourages un-silence.

Tell us about your first time reading at Neo and do you remember what poem you read (if so what was the name)?

First time at Neo I read "Self Acceptance: An Open Letter from the Pot to the Kettle"—What I remember most is meeting Brian Francis and how he treated me like I was already family. Tumblr: www.BeingGlori.tumblr.com.

97

Kelene Blake-Fallon

How long have you been writing/performing poetry?
22 years writing. 6 years performing.

How would you describe your style of poetry?
Honest, like the sea, sometimes gentle and healing, sometimes dangerous.

What is your favorite thing about poetry?
The structure and lack of structure. The ability to paint your words with creative brush strokes.

Tell us about your first time reading at Neo and do you remember what poem you read (if so what was the name)?
I was hanging out with Jewlz. She told BFran I should get on the mic. BFran profiled me, thought I would be a total newbie, but I had my poem memorized and ready. My first poem at Neo was "Revolutions."

Joe "Element615" Brundidge

How long have you been writing/performing poetry?

I've been writing since I was a kid; performing since I was 20.

How would you describe your style of poetry?

Prose when it needs to be, rhyme when it has to, with its own structure regardless. It goes where it needs to.

What is your favorite thing about poetry?

That it's a lifetime in an instant.

Tell us about your first time reading at Neo and do you remember what poem you read (if so what was the name)?

Neo felt like the place I needed to be, at a time I needed that. I read a poem called "The Family Man."

Julian "Professor J"

How long have you been writing/performing poetry?

I've been writing poetry since middle school, but honestly it started off as love letters to failed romances. I started slamming about 4 years ago.

How would you describe your style of poetry?

I would describe my poetry style as the backwash of a beer left out in the heat, a tablespoon of Robitussin, or a well shot on Sunday morning. My poetry style is rough to swallow and doesn't sit well in your chest. I try to stick as close as I can to the actual environment the poem originated from (whether good or bad) to help me have the same emotion I first had when I encountered that experience growing up. Most of the time, my poems center around a negative experience I had growing up or speaking on the Mexican experience from both sides of the border that major news stations don't dare talk about.

What is your favorite thing about poetry?

What I love about poetry is that it can be treated as an art form or as a form of therapy. I see it as both, but primarily as therapy. I started to heavily rely on poetry when I was struggling to fit in the college atmosphere as a first generation Mexican-American college student. What I love about poetry the most is that it took me out of very depressive years as a college student.

Tell us about your first time reading at Neo and do you remember what poem you read (if so what was the name)?

The first time I read at Neo, I believe it was an open mic night. I wasn't sure if I wanted to stick to slam poetry after slamming at Austin Poetry Slam and feeling like I wasn't up to par with the rest of the poets. If it weren't for Brian Francis and Danny Strack coming up to me (on separate occasions) and genuinely expressing interest in my poetry and saying "hello" on my first night of slam poetry (for each venue) I think I would have called it quits right away. I'm glad I can call Danny a really good friend of mine as well as my poetry mentor and Brian Francis a coach and teammate, but most importantly, I get to call them family. If I remember correctly, one of the first poems I ever started with was a poem about my mother and knowing I would lose her one day. It's a very heartfelt piece that I feel a lot of people connect to, but it's a poem I don't like performing much because I always feel like breaking down in the middle of the performance. Instagram: @jcopado10; Twitter: @JulianCopado.

John Crow

How long have you been writing/performing poetry?

I would say my official start was in 1997, or at least that's when I began to put real effort into writing. I owe my start to Cocoa Fire. She was the first poet I ever heard do what I had always done in my head, out loud.

How would you describe your style of poetry?

Now it's mostly political satire and commentary. Although I enjoy a good Haiku, I've never been a person to write too metaphorically. I write what I feel. Sometimes it's only in my head, but in my head it's the voice of GOD.

What is your favorite thing about poetry?

I like hearing new people, first timers find their voice. I love that anyone can write about life the way they see it.

Tell us about your first time reading at Neo and do you remember what poem you read (if so what was the name)?

Wow that's tough. I remember Neo before slam, when the open mic was all we had. I miss that. Back then, we were closer as a community. Killeen would roll 5-10 car loads deep. Neo Souljas were a hoard! I think the first poem I spit at Neo was called "Already Met;" it came to be known as the back and the crack poem. That was

101

my signature poem for a long time. I was nervous and BFran hugged me and with confidence in his eyes he said, "Spit Poet! I HEAR YA!" I still hear him in my head. It's crowded in there. Facebook: John Crow; Twitter: @JohnCrow.

Sunni Soper

How long have you been writing/performing poetry?

I wrote my first poem in October 2010, but didn't share one until I found NeoSoul Poetry Lounge at Midtown in 2013.

How would you describe your style of poetry?

I would describe my poetry as rhythmic and conversational, mostly streams of consciousness. I'm a dreamer.

What is your favorite thing about poetry?

I love the people it has brought into my life and the avenue it gives me to reach others to open them up and get them expressing themselves. I love that poetry lets me sit down with a problem, have a conversation with myself, then get up from the table and leave it on the paper. Or the stage. Or burn it. Whichever therapy the problem asks for.

Tell us about your first time reading at Neo and do you remember what poem you read (if so what was the name)?

I found out about Neo at an R&B artist's show. Shae and Kelene opened up for him and I was blown away. I came back the next Tuesday (February 19, 2013) and accidentally entered a slam. I thought the word 'slam' was just code for a poetry open mic; I learned in about 15 minutes how mistaken I was. I read a piece called "Naked Yet Clothed," written specifically for my first time reading a poem out loud. The rest is herstory. www.sunnisoperpoetry.com; Facebook: Sunni Soper; Twitter/Instagram: @SunniThaPoet.

Shanitria "Shae" Harris

A born and raised Austinite who spent her youth competing nationally in spoken word. Since her multiple Youth Slam Champ wins, she has progressed to be one of the most powerful female voices in the Austin poetry community. After competing nationally at NPS, Shae lead the 2013 Austin NeoSoul team to first place in the nation in group piece poems. Wanting to take a more supporting role, she is currently the Director of Operations for Austin NeoSoul Poetry Lounge, and can be found working behind the scenes magic for Austin's longest running open mic. She is currently finishing her Master's Degree in Legal Studies at Texas State University and her first self published book "Ether."

SLAM THEIRSTORY

NeoSoul has been participating in the National Poetry Slam (NPS) Championship since 2006 and in that time, they have established themselves as a national poetic power.

2006
Inaugural National Poetry Slam: 2006
Team: Michelle Desiree, Thirteen, Trey Stepter, Element 615 (Joe B), and Brian Francis
Coach: Mike Whalen

Finals, 2nd in the Nation
Austin, Texas.

2007
Team: Michelle Desiree, Faylita Hicks, Ms. Lizz, Element 615, Ebony Stewart
Coach Brian Francis

Semifinals, 20th in the Nation
Austin, Texas.

2008

Team: Michelle Desiree, Korim, Faylita Hicks, and Brian Francis

Coach: Thirteen

Semifinals 14th in the Nation, Madison, Wisconsin.

2009
Team: Jomar Valentin, Cousin Sarah,
Tova Charles and Ebony Stewart
Coach: Brian Francis

Semifinal 15th in the nation
West Palm Beach, Florida.

2010
Austin NeoSoul Team 2010
Team: Scottfree, Ebony Stewart, Zai, Jomar
Valentin, and Brently Caballero
Coach: Brian Francis

Final, 4th in the Nation
St.Paul, Minnesota.

#ebonyshirt

2011

Team: Zai, Scottfree, Allen Small, Ebony Stewart and Brian Francis
Coaches: Thirteen and Mike Whalen

Group Piece Final, 3rd Place
Boston, Massachusetts.

2012
Team: Zai, Korim, LaLove, Danny Strack, and Shae
Coaches: Ebony Stewart and Brian Francis

Group Piece Finals , 1st Place
Charlotte, North Carolina.

2013
Team: Glori B, Jacob Dodson, Margaret Ruth
Olson, Victoria Murray, and Doc
Coaches: Brian Francis and Jomar Valentin

Group Piece Finals 1st Place
Haiku Deathmatch Champion, Glori B.
Boston, Massachusetts.

2014
Team: Doc, Brian Francis, Scottfree, Kayla Q,
Teresa Johnson and Kelene Blake
Coaches: Brian Francis and Victoria Murray

Group Piece Finals, 2nd Place
Oakland, California

2015
Team: Jomar Valentin, Christopher Michael,
Brian Francis, Doc and Teresa Johnson
Coach: Tova Charles

Group Piece Finals, 3rd Place
Oakland, California

2016
Team: Teresa Johnson, Brian Francis, Glori B, Julian Copado, John Crow
Coach: Christopher Michael

Finals: 4th in the Nation
Haiku Deathmatch Champion: Glori B.
Decatur, Georgia.

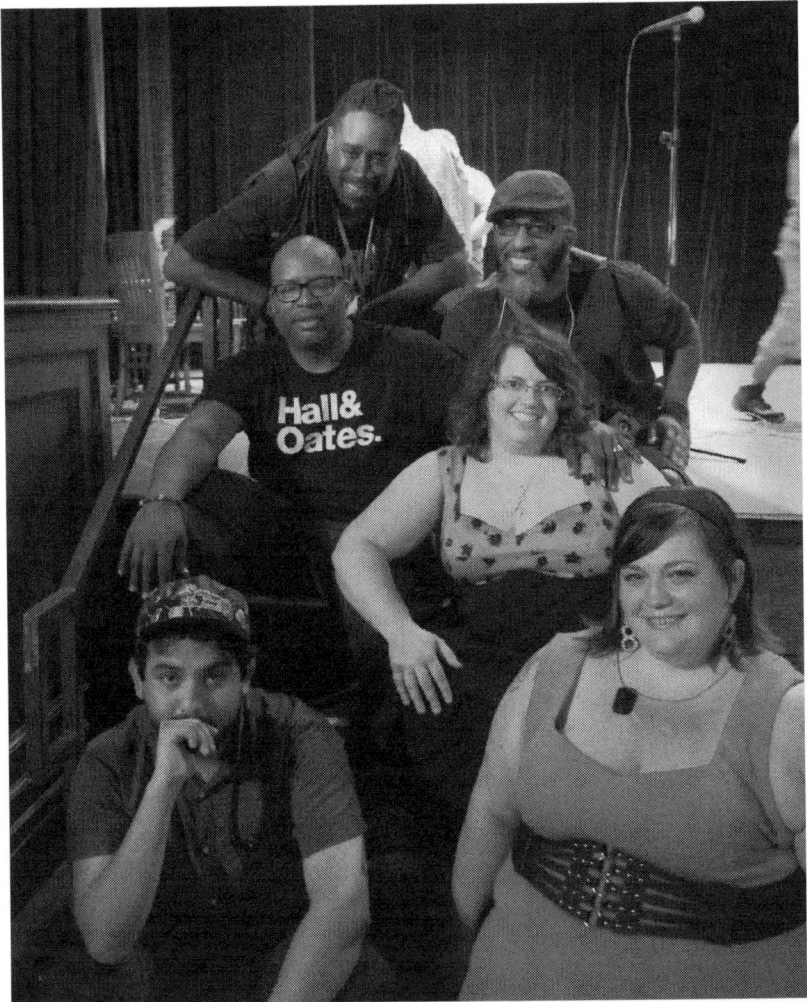

The Pens Of NeoSoul Poetry Slam

310 BROWN STREET .com

f @neosoulatx

neoSoul poetry ATX est. 2005

The Anthology

From The Pens Of NeoSoul Poetry Slam

vol: one

Austin NeoSoul

Made in the USA
San Bernardino, CA
18 August 2017